a girl's guide to

glamour

a girl's guide to
glamour

sandra deeble

illustrations by *chris long*

RYLAND
PETERS
& SMALL

LONDON NEW YORK

Designer Sonya Nathoo
Editor Miriam Hyslop
Production Manager Patricia Harrington
Art Director Gabriella Le Grazie
Publishing Director Alison Starling

First published in the United States
in 2005 by Ryland Peters & Small, Inc.
519 Broadway
5th Floor
New York, NY 10012
www.rylandpeters.com

Text, design, and illustrations
© Ryland Peters & Small 2005

10 9 8 7 6 5 4 3 2 1

Printed and bound in China.

ISBN 1 84172 859 4

contents

introduction

Glamour is a way of being—upbeat and aspirational with an untouchable magnetism. Glamour can sometimes be easy to spot. Glamour commands attention. Perfect fire red lips. A silver compact. A dry martini. Sleek black tie. It has an unfettered style that is compelling and desirable. Glamour is a sophisticated whirling cocktail of worldliness, adventure, and daring, anchored by an enigmatic blend of beauty and allure.

Glamour comes from within. It's a state of mind. Certainly, you can treat glamour as an accessory and bring it on when the mood takes you. I took to wearing a little black dress while writing this book and, come early evening, my desk was often graced with a glass of champagne. Yet true glamour goes deeper than that. Whenever I posed the question "What is glamour?" I was always well rewarded: "It's innate." "It's aspirational escapism." "You're born with it." "You don't have to be beautiful." "We've all got it in us."

Glamour has old-world, Hollywood screen goddess connotations. You can bet your life that at a party during the 1930s or 1940s nobody would have wasted a second pondering the meaning of glamour. Hell, no. They were far too busy living and breathing glamour. They had no doubt about how to be glamorous. They WERE glamorous.

Glamour has always been with us—simmering under the surface of grunge and other equally lackadaisical statements. Yet there has never been a greater need to celebrate the gorgeousness of glamour. We need to offset the seriousness and stresses of modern life with the fizz of frivolous fun. We hanker after glamour—so often in a retro way because modern glamour is ill defined. I trust this guide will give you the confidence and the wherewithal to find a glamour that fits comfortably—obviously not too comfortably, because comfy isn't glamorous— with who you are and how you live.

So, if you're ready—and you might want to take a moment to check your lipstick in your silver compact—I would like to invite you to join me as we embark on a stylish voyage of rediscovery to capture the spirit of glamour, and master the art of true va-va-voom.

inner *glamour*

Glamour is more than skin-deep—it starts in the mind. The key to unlocking your inner voluptuousness is simple: confidence, confidence, confidence. Repeat after me: I am gorgeous. I glow. I have glamour.

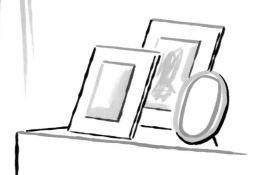

it's all in the mind

I am gorgeous. I glow. I have glamour.

You might like to pause for a moment, mid-mantra. Saying it is one thing, believing it is another. Going into a trance-like glamorous state won't necessarily make you start looking like Charlize Theron or Halle Berry. Yet the really great thing about glamour is that it is possible to think yourself glamorous. Here are some tips to get you started.

Think glamour

* ✱ Shed doubts now.
* ✱ Stop wondering what other people think about you.
* ✱ Close your eyes and visualize yourself in a world where you float, breathe evenly, and your heart beats firmly yet calmly. Say to yourself that you are 100 per cent certain that your place in the world is admired, welcomed, and envied. Believe it.
* ✱ Hypnotize yourself if you can—play haunting music—and see yourself living out a soignée life in rapturous Technicolor.
* ✱ Be kind to yourself. If there are areas of your life that are lackluster or in disarray, make time to think about them. Don't panic. Your mind doesn't need to spiral out of control.
* ✱ Start practicing a more glamorous vocabulary—from today.
* ✱ Luxuriate in your life, revel in the good things, sparkle in company, fizz with laughter, celebrate hedonism, fun, and joy.

know thyself

In order to garner glamour, you need to bare all—to yourself.
A life unexamined is a life not worth living, believed Socrates, but
a body unexamined will not help you to live life to the full.

You need to be honest. Kindly so, rather than brutally honest. Don't be
so frank with yourself that you end up in a sobbing heap on the floor
(along with all those clothes you've discarded in a fit of pique because
you've suddenly realized they do nothing for you).

Having confidence in yourself is gained from making the best of your
raw ingredients. Be aware of both your strengths and not-so-feisty
features, then deal with reality. As a rule of thumb, flaunt the fabulous,
disguise the disappointing. If you recognize any of the following, here
are some suggestions to help you to become a master of disguises:

Large breasts
Yes: Wide and low necklines. **No:** Halter or high necks.

Love handles
Yes: Flares. **No:** Baggy tops, hipsters.

Thick ankles
Yes: Long skirts. **No:** Capri pants, kitten heels.

Plump arms

Yes: Hide. Go for floaty sleeves. **No:** Cap sleeves, skin-tight long sleeves, spaghetti straps.

Flat chests

Yes: Halter and high necks. **No:** Round t-shirts under V-neck tops.

I know my bum looks big

Yes: Flared skirted jackets that cover critical area. **No:** Short jackets, A-line skirts.

Overhang tummy

Yes: Ballet-style wrap tops, Jane Austen Empire dresses. **No:** Hipsters (sorry about this).

Thick waist

Yes: Low plunge V necks, cut off cardigans. **No:** Double-breasted anything, shift dresses, baggy pullovers.

Short legs

Yes: Just-below-knee skirts, layered tops. In summer, skin-tone shoes (this tip comes from Marilyn Monroe). Looks very odd in winter with dark clothes, obviously. **No:** Crop tops, mid-calf skirts.

tips for inner glamour

There are those who believe that glamour has no place in macrobiotic diets, or with green tea, Bikram yoga, early nights and 2$^1/_2$ quarts of water a day. I disagree.

Inside-out glamour endures. Lipstick wears off but the glow that comes from feeling happy in your skin is worth its weight in pumpkin seeds. The trick is not to be glum. Balance is key. To get started, here are my top tips for nurturing inner glamour:

Drink water
Tap, bottled, whatever. Lots of it. I know it's boring, I know you've heard it before, but just drink it. By the time we get to the obligatory cocktails, you'll be well and truly pretoxed.

Sleep
Sultry sirens enjoy heavenly repose. Invest in a good spring mattress. Wallow in a candlelit lavender bath. Create a pleasure zone: sensual boudoir meets chamber of calm.

Eat
Think purifying, think energizing, think packed with the good stuff. Oily fish. Greens and beans. Blue, red, and orange foods—they're anti-aging. Minimize caffeine, fat, sugar, and anything processed.

Stretch

Yoga, Pilates, swimming, walking, or good old-fashioned calisthenics. Get as much fresh air as you can. Glamour walks tall.

Dream

By day and by night. Allow yourself a sacrosanct morsel of time alone to let your mind wander wherever it likes.

Be good

Look after yourself. I will refrain from saying "Treat your body like a temple" but show your appreciation and it'll serve you well.

Be bad

If you feel rejuvenated just knowing that you can manage on three hours sleep, after dancing till dawn, then do it. We need lightness in life. Be mad. It's good for the soul.

Detox your mind

Worry is hellishly aging. Do what you need to—seek help, talk to friends, deal with the past, and move on.

Meditate

Learn how to. Serenity is divine.

golden rules
of glamour

The key to glamour is making your efforts look and feel effortless. In this chapter we will take a look at some inspiring icons from Ava Gardner to Katharine Hepburn, harness the not-so-elusive capsule wardrobe, and get to grips with the golden rules of glamour.

glamour types

Glamour is accessible to all of us. Here are some glamorous women we can admire and capture some of their "look."

Showy starlet with hourglass figure
Who: Ava Gardner, Rita Hayworth
How: Work on your eyebrows. Arch them as far as they will go. Wear divine dresses of slinky mermaid proportions. Accentuate your hips. Wear belts. Think cinch.

Platinum blonde screen goddess
Who: Marilyn Monroe, Scarlett Johansson, Charlize Theron
How: Become blonde if you're not already. Experiment with different voices—try gravely or breathy. Recline on a chaise longue.

Smoky sultry siren
Who: Marlene Dietrich, Uma Thurman, Sophia Loren
How: Smudge taupe shadow on your lids to get the "smoky eye" look. Perfect a slightly dangerous come-hither look.

Sophisticated elegance
Who: Audrey Hepburn, Grace Kelly
How: Wear over-sized sunglasses (essential). Pearls. Black turtle neck sweater. Little black dress. Long gloves. A headscarf.

the capsule wardrobe

Achievable objective or urban myth? The capsule wardrobe is within the grasp of us all. Get it right and it'll save you time, money, and energy spent wondering about what to wear. It'll greatly reduce those wrinkly frowns developing on your brow as you despairingly sort through the pile of clothes on your bed. Glamour has a smooth, untroubled forehead.

How to do it

Grab some refuse bags. Set aside half a day. Ask a friend to help, then celebrate over lunch and a bottle of pink Perrier Jouet.

Start with a color. Any color. Oh, all right, black if you must. But navy can work as a basis, if that's your thing. As can brown.

Ask yourself (and your friend) the following questions about each item: Does it fit? Is it a flattering friend or foe? What does it go with?

Be ruthless. If there are things you haven't worn for a hundred years but the fabric is laden with nostalgia, then keep a swatch and make a kind of keepsake in a photo album. Don't over-butcher items because you will take all unwanted clothes to your favorite thrift store.
You've now got your base color and you've done the cull. Well done.
Crack open that champagne and enjoy the next bit.

Every girl needs…

What you're aiming for is your own spin on the following:

* Three skirts (short, knee, long).
* Three pairs of trousers (day, evening, and jeans or something very casual if you don't like jeans).
* Three pairs of shoes (day, evening, and boots).
* One jacket (goes with one skirt to make a suit).
* Shirts that go with all of the above.
* One little black dress.
* Trench coat or raincoat.
* Stunningly elegant winter coat, classic rather than fashion item— I've got one I've had for years and every season I get cascades of compliments.
* No more than five items that you love and still wear but that don't necessarily go with anything else.

There will be other paraphernalia:
Flip-flops, sandals, swimsuits, wraps, walking-in-rain garb, and accessories which we'll be looking at next. I believe the the key to the capsule wardrobe is this: be totally confident that everything you own really does make you feel and look your very best. Love what's in your wardrobe and wear everything in it. Then wait for the compliments to start coming your way.

Storage hints

* Hang clothes according to weight. Light and floaty things together. Heavy coats and jackets together.
* Store bias-cut clothes in boxes with tissue paper. If they hang for years, they get skewed.
* Keep shoes in clear boxes. Some people go for Polaroids stuck on the outside. Mere mortals probably don't need to go this far.

Accessories

The best accessories have a tale to tell. The clutch bag that ended up in someone else's flat or spent the night in a black cab. The dangly earring that got caught in someone else's shrug and went off on a little adventure to a new part of town. The shoes that danced the night away and were loved and admired by all.

Accessories speak volumes. Money can buy accessories, but if your salary is not princely—or princessy—take heart. While I'm not going to suggest that you pop down to the cheapest stores, there are ways of mixing and matching and being clever.

Sole to sole

"Give a girl the right shoes and she can conquer the world," Bette Midler once said. How true. The harsh reality is that most of us haven't got cupboards full of Manolo Blahnik, Gina, and Jimmy Choo boxes.

It doesn't matter. All you need is quality—shoes that are well made and that fit well. Pamper them, polish them, and remember that glamour is well heeled, so you need to find a good shoe repair store and bond with them. If you want to apply the capsule philosophy to footwear, here's how you do it:

* One pair of loafers or flat shoes.
* One pair of sensible dress shoes or low-heeled shoes.
* One pair of girl-about-town evening shoes (and these could be your drop-dead designer stilettos—Christian Louboutin or Sergio Rossi or Beatrix Ong or whoever you happen to love).
* One pair of knee-length boots.

Bag lady

Anya Hindmarch? Lulu Guinness? Fendi? Prada? You can get seriously bogged down with bags. Personally, I believe that glamour stems from simplicity: reduce confusion and clutter in life.

Dreaming about designer bags can seriously interfere with your beauty sleep. Whether you're captivated by an alligator-skin doctor's bag or a clutch bag that looks like a flamenco fan, the reality is that you really can live well with three bags:

* The Work Bag—Big, but not too big. You'll ruin your posture if it's too heavy. Neutral rather than matching. Leather totes are good workhorses—they're great for working girls and also for mothers who carry piles of baby stuff.
* The Weekend Bag—Time to shrug off that work bag. Softer materials: canvas, nylon, linen, silk, raffia. When you pick up this bag to go out you'll be so happy to leave your weekday satchel behind.
* The Out-on-the-Town-Bag—Did I really say ONE of these? I have friends who amass mini clutch bags with the fervor of stamp collectors. And vintage bags are wonderful to collect—and use. Whether you go for bag museum or minimalism, ask yourself if it will take your phone, credit card, keys, and cash.

And yes, size does matter. Particularly for work and weekend bags, think about balance, according to your size and height. More importantly—graceful is best. Buy a smaller bag than you'll think you'll need, then force yourself to carry the bare minimum.

shopping

Target or Manolo? Goodwill or Oscar de la Renta? Gucci or Gap?
The big luxury brands have been embraced by the masses and have
subsequently lost their chic. This is good news for the less than
loaded. Thrift style is exclusive. It's almost subversive, with the rich
opting for factory outlet jeans or Wallmart over Earl Jean, Burberry,
and Fendi.

Glamour needs to be individual. Nobody wants cookie-cutter, look-
alike glamour, so I would like each and every one of you to start
shopping smartly.

Combine clothes in unexpected ways—department store and vintage
with designer and something you've customized yourself at home.

Don't worry about being dressed in the next thing or trying to be ahead
of the game when it comes to fashion. There are no winners—only
sad, confused, and exhausted people.

Instead, remember how to be glamorous within. Know your strengths
and play to them. Shop for fun and enjoy the journey. And make sure
you stop for lunch—and a cocktail or two.

high maintenance

A beautiful patina is one thing. But favorite items of clothing shouldn't look tired. Look after your things and as a result YOU will feel pampered. Trust me. It works.

Celebrating domesticity has a certain sexiness. Just-ironed laundry and recently reheeled shoes can rekindle the new relationship, butterflies-in-stomach feelings you had when you first bought them.

A stitch in time
Repair coat linings. Reinforce any dangling labels right away. A button missing doesn't even bear thinking about.

Lustrous leather
Feed it. Don't store leather bags or belts near a radiator or hot pipes.

Get stuffing
Stuff shoes and bags with crumpled up paper when they're resting.

Dry cleaning
As a rule of thumb, avoid buying clothes that need dry cleaning but inevitably you'll still have to schlep to the dry cleaners more often than is good for you. But enjoy collecting your dry cleaning as everything will have a new-car feel-good factor.

Ironing

Enjoy it. Invest in scented waters for linen water and buy a state-of-the-art iron and board—or even a designer cover.

Well heeled

Leather—find a good worker and develop a bond. Ditto a tailor or seamstress. If you're ever stuck with broken leather belts, bags, and handles, try to find a good leather repair shop.

Laundry

Glamour is sweet smelling and well creased, rather like the edge of Cary Grant's jaw. Enjoy caring for your clothes. Buy gentle eco-friendly detergents for handwashing, and invest in chunky baskets and wooden clothespins for hanging out.

Storage

Invest in beautiful hangers. Grow lavender—even if it's in a window box—and make your own lavender bags.

Disasters

If you ever have a disaster with a much loved item of clothing years after you've bought it, try going back to the manufacturer for help, rather than the store.

beauty

Glamour owes a hell of a lot to health and well-being. If you make yourself feel splendid, it will resonate and you will exude The Glow.

Pampering
Cherish yourself. Have manicures, pedicures, facials, massages. If you don't have the budget to go out and be pampered, you will have to be disciplined and make time for yourself at home. Have your eyebrows done professionally and the whole of you will feel more soignée.

Perfume
Glamour is always fragrant. A dressing table laden with myriad perfume bottles is all well and good, but I am an advocate of having your own individual scent. Find something natural that suits you and that enhances your own true spirit.

Make-up
Here's what you need for a capsule make-up bag:
* Two foundations: full on for winter, light for summer.
* Two lipsticks, day and night.
* One lip pencil.
* One blusher.
* One mascara.
* One eye and brow pencil.

emergency glamour

Stockings with a run have no place in glamour. What every girl needs is a First Aid Kit for those moments when glamour flees and leaves you high and dry.

First aid

* An extra pair of stockings.
* An emery board.
* Nail polish if you're wearing it, just in case you do something silly and unglam like chip or break a nail.
* Mini shoe-shine kit that you collect from a hotel.
* Miniature sewing kit—also from hotel.
* Water. Keep drinking it.
* Stop! Breathe. There's nothing like it. Deep breathing will always come to your aid and help you rescue glamour.
* Nap when possible. Mandatory for homeworkers. I think all office workers should observe the siesta—it's life-enhancing.
* Always make sure you have your result outfit clean and ready to go.
* Keep miniature bottles of champagne in the fridge—you never know when you'll need a pick-me-up.
* If you're out and about and suddenly feel slumpy and unglamorous, go to your nearest hip hotel and make full use of the facilities. Even if you just sit in the lobby and have a glass of spring water, I guarantee it'll restore glamour in no time.

glamour for free

Wonderful, wonderful news! Glamour can be gratis. Yes indeedy. If you're in the know, you will find it easy to garner glamour with alacrity and for next to nothing. If you ever feel a bit raggedy— and God knows we all do sometimes—here are some simple, cheap and cheerful ways to be more glamorous for free.

Here's the thing. You might be slumped at home, and slumping might be the very pose that reflects your state of mind. Yet at the same time you should know that it's easy as pie to bring on outfits, music, and a touch of madness to change your mood before you can say "Glamracadrabra"!

Going out

* Step out with confidence and set off for a jewelry store— preferably one that looks dangerously expensive. Look, and better still, try on without buying—very *Breakfast at Tiffany's*.
* The same goes for the hippest of boutiques. Never feel intimidated by so-called glam store assistants. Remember: you have your own inner glamour. Enjoy it!
* Go to a vintage store and revel in beauty.
* Head for a lingerie emporium and do more wafting. Look for Myla, La Perla, or Rigby and Peller. After this, hit some department stores and see what you're more likely to be able to afford.

Staying in

* Clean your home as if the Queen—or someone you really admire—were coming to visit.
* Fill it with tulips.
* Spend an indulgent hour or two browsing through old photos to see whether you are looking particularly glamorous in any of them. Enjoy wallowing in the memories of any sparkling moments and toy with the idea of recapturing your glam inner teenager.
* Shed your cleaning clothes while running a bath filled with the oil or bubbles you keep for best. Transform your bathroom into a boudoir simply by filling it with church candles. Sink into deliciously perfumed water with a soft purr.
* Pamper your body as if you were getting ready for a Third Date. Leave no elbow unexfoliated. Skin should feel sensual and you should feel truly gorgeous.
* Curl up—or perch sedately—on the sofa with a stash of old films. Anything with Lauren Bacall or Audrey Hepburn will fit the bill nicely.
* Arm yourself with that box of truffles you've been saving as if—for a rainy day.
* Paint your nails a glossy shade of plum.
* Practice painting your lips fire-engine red—then perfect your pout in front of a mirror.

deportment

"Audrey Hepburn's stance is a combination of an ultra fashion plate and a ballet dancer," Cecil Beaton wrote in the October 1954 issue of Vogue. *He also talked about her "rod-like back" and "long, incredibly slender and straight neck."*

Fair enough. If you're lucky, you'll have giraffe ancestors. If not, and you have been landed with a rather short, pudgy neck, do not despair. The good news is that the rod-like back and a ballerina stance is achievable by one and all. And remember: giraffes don't really cut it on the dance floor.

Here's how

5 top activities to help you on your way to achieving ballet dancer deportment:

* Alexander technique—excellent for all kinds of things, including public speaking and generally helping you to gain the poise and confidence to float through life.
* Pilates—a winner. Strengthens, tones, and gets that stomach squashed once and for all.
* Yoga—choose a brand that suits you: Ashtanga, Bikram, whatever.
* Dancing—salsa, ceroc, jitterbug, tango, tap, ballet.
* Hiking—you could join the Sierra Club. Or not.

everyday
glamour

Don't save glamour for special occasions and holidays. You might not feel you can handle a full-blown red-carpet vamped-up lifestyle, but at the same time I am a great advocate of allowing micro moments of glamour to spice up the quotidian.

glamour at work

"Glamour is what I sell. It's my stock in trade." Marlene Dietrich.
*I'm not suggesting that you make a career out of glamour. However,
I do know from experience that office politics take on a whole new
meaning if you strut around the workplace looking like Eva Peron.*

Forget power dressing. We're talking style, femininity, playing to your
strengths, and oozing authority and charm. People will start to look to
you when they want an opinion. Look and feel glamorous when you're
at your day job and I promise you that you'll never worry about
work/life balance issues again. I'm not talking old-school secretarial
eyelash fluttering; what I'm saying is that if you feel fabulous when
you're at work, everything you want will flow towards you: money,
interesting projects, opportunities, the works. Here's how to do it:

By day

Be smart, very smart. You might work in a loft somewhere doing clever
things with content and codes and flash—if so, I'm sure you'll know
whatever fits best in an incredibly high-octane techno trendy
environment. But, for more traditional workplaces:

* Herringbone linen dresses and kitten heels in summer.
* Quality—the best you can afford because you'll be getting far more
  wear out of work clothes than anything else in your wardrobe.
* Neutral tones—you can forgo black every so often.

* Slacks (Armani-esque without necessarily being Armani).
* Prada sport shoes (again without being Prada).
* Drink water (sorry to go on about this)—it'll stop you feeling limp.
* Eat fruit and seeds (pumpkin and sunflower) for perky energy.
  Glamour doesn't flag.
* Take a brisk constitutional at lunchtime, whatever the weather.

After hours

Have you ever been feeling grim and crumpled and longing to get
home and soak in the bath when you get an impromptu invitation
to something quite glitzy? Do not despair. You need to create a Day-
to-Night Kit. This should contain:

* A top that sparkles and can be worn under your work jacket
  to be revealed once you arrive at the event.
* Another pair of shoes—higher, sexier, more evening.
* Tiny evening bag (decant phone, cash, credit card, keys, and lipstick,
  and leave the rest of your stuff at work in your work bag).
* Make-up remover and all that you need to apply a fresh face.
  Keep all this in a drawer in your desk in miniature bottles.
* Travel toothbrush and tiny tube of toothpaste.
* If you have time, and if you work near shops get yourself to
  a department store for a complete makeover—for free.

glamour at home

Working from home hasn't traditionally been conducive to glamour. Isn't part of the joy of homeworking being able to please yourself? Perhaps this is why "Do you work in your pyjamas?" is the question I'm forced to answer at least once a week. But I think that there's a certain kind of "glam loafing" or luxurious lounging that can and should begin at home. And not just when you're getting glammed up to go out.

Work from home in your pyjamas by all means, but make sure that they are in jewel colors and made of silk. An alternative is white or soft-cream-colored linen. If you're feeling chilly, throw on an organza or chiffon wrap, or perhaps a beautifully beaded sweater. In winter, velvet and cashmere take to the stage. I often complete this look with sequinned Moroccan slippers which, every now and then, I shrug off to reveal my exquisitely exfoliated feet and perfectly pedicured toes.

I do realize that unexpected guests—who I now welcome with open arms because I'm always looking my best—might question whether I'm redefining myself as a Holly Golightly for the noughties or even freelancing for Hugh Hefner, but I stick to my guns. I feel at home with my penchant for luxurious lounging and let me tell you that working from home is now a lot more fun.

If you'd like to have a go at glam loafing, here are some do's and don'ts.

Don't

* Wear clothes more suited to the gym or jogging.
* EVER have potpourri in bowls.
* Loaf around without make-up.
* Have bad-hair days or wear a scrunchie.
* Leave dirty dishes in the sink.
* Indulge in general slovenly sloppiness.

Do

* Watch old films in the afternoon.
* Wear a tiara.
* Plump cushions.
* Have blowsy blooms all over the place.
* Take to your bed whenever you feel like it—eye mask is optional.
* Have a bathroom of hip hotel standards.
* Enjoy being the charming hostess.
* Light candles—church ones or naturally scented.
* Observe the Cocktail Hour. From six onwards it's time to up the ante. I like to change into something different: a little black dress and heels, or a pair of smart slacks, and a plain sweater. Sip a Peach Bellini in summer, or a martini in winter.

weekend glamour

Weekends can be tricky. For every 1,000 badly dressed, unglamorous, unkempt girls out shopping at the weekend there will be one clever girl who has thought about her splurge and dressed to please—herself.

Success breeds success. Glamour breeds glamour. If you make an effort—especially if you're going out to buy clothes, shoes, or make-up—you will make better and more glamorous choices. I actually think that the key at weekends is not to step out thinking, "I hope to God I don't bump into someone I know", but "I am ready for an impromptu chat with anyone I happen to meet."

Meeting friends for lunch

Or brunch. I know that by mentioning *SATC* I will sound like a person who has totally lost a grip. We've cried, we've had closure, we've moved on. But I used to love the brunches and while there was the odd occasion when Carrie frankly looked—well, almost unwashed and definitely washed out—there were myriad occasions when they all looked fabulous. And probably felt fabulous.

Walk in the park or the countryside

You could think Central Park in the fall with well-coordinated outfit but frankly that's trying too hard. Then there's always the fancy-dress shooting party get-up. You choose.

holidays

Style is the most compatible traveling companion for glamour. Please remember this: just because you're on vacation it doesn't mean you can forget about glamour and let yourself go. Relax, by all means, but please do not let standards slip.

Hip places change constantly according to whims of fashion but here are a few destinations which I think you'll agree will be forever glamorous:

* French Riviera—racy, dangerous, seductive. Think Cary Grant in *To Catch a Thief*.
* Miami—pink hotels, pink drinks, what more can you ask for?
* LA—Rodeo Drive, shopping paradise.
* Rome—Vespas, espresso—heaven.
* Milan—Prada. Do you need anything else?
* Home—your own. Staying at home is part of the new "vacation every day" movement.
* Trans-Siberian Express or Trans-Canadian—or any other long-distance train journey. Think Eva Marie Saint in *North by Northwest*.
* San Francisco—Notting Hill with cable cars.
* Zanzibar—it just sounds glam.
* Pantelleria—ditto.
* North Island, Seychelles—location for Tracy Island in *Thunderbirds*. Lady Penelope will always have glamour.

Luggage

This used to be so simple. It is now a minefield. A complete Louis Vuitton trunk set used to be *le plus ultra*. Sadly, Vuitton is one of those luxury brands that has been slightly debased. You'll have to think again. Samsonite is too business-like and Mulberry too house party. You could go modern and opt for Mandarina Duck. Or, better still, go no brand. Find an exquisite leather carryall or suitcases in soft bitter-chocolate leather made by an unknown Italian craftsman. Everyone will beg you to tell them where they can get the same but you will merely smile enigmatically as you sashay along to rest your pins in the first-class lounge.

Packing

Many glamorous women eschew the minimalist packing approach, preferring to pack according to planned activities. Linen dress, hat, and raffia bag for galleries. Capri pants for arriving at beach. Lace-up corset to wear over vintage flowing dress with fake diamond bracelet for first-night aperitif at hotel bar. I've never put this to the test to see which approach ends up creating the most luggage. You might like to try it. Other top tips for packing include: rolling clothes into sausages, packing delicate fabrics in dry-cleaning bags or in tissue paper, and buying tiny decanters for all beauty products.

How to be a smart packer for a beach holiday:

* Big sunglasses—this goes without saying.
* Cardigan—1950s style with brooch, or noughties style: beaded, sequinned or both.
* One or two crinkly dresses.
* Linen drawstring pajama bottoms.
* Smart pants—linen or cotton.
* Linen shirts.
* One white T-shirt or sleeveless top for every day you're away.
* Kaftan and turban for that Agatha Christie murder look.
* Sarong (if you can't face a kaftan).
* Birkenstocks or equivalent.
* Minimal beach-friendly jewelry.
* Strappy sundress.
* Elegant but not-too-high-to-walk-in shoes. If you want to take heels, take heels. But don't pack five pairs of shoes. Don't.
* Swimsuit or bikini or both.
* Floppy hat.
* Beach bag.
* Smaller evening bag.
* Pashmina/wrap—could be useful on the plane.

evening out
glamour

Sequins, sparkles, frivolity, anticipation, nerves, moonlight, mystery. Bring it on. Getting glammed up for a night out is not just a question of ruby lipstick, lip gloss, and a cloud of perfume. It's far more subtle than that.

dress to seduce

Now we're talking. Every woman should ideally attend an Art of Seduction evening class to really excel in this area but feeling and looking the part goes almost all the way. With any luck, you'll already have a 'result' dress or outfit. It goes without saying that the nature of the desired result can vary from person to person.

Dressing to seduce is a wondrous art. Carrying it off—the seduction—necessitates a warm blend of glamour, style, sex appeal and panache. If you're dressing to seduce on a school night, that is a pity, and I'm afraid you'll have to adapt this advice.

Plan
Plan it within an inch of your life and enjoy every minute of the getting-ready process.

Pamper yourself
Ideally, take the whole day to gear up to the bathing and dressing stage, but make it a slow, rolling boil. Exfoliation, deep hair treatments, body wraps, face masks, afternoon nap, hydrate your system with herbal tea and water.

Seductive thoughts

While you're getting ready—from bathtime to the final slick of lip gloss—think affirming thoughts about your sexuality and expertise in the art of erotic striptease. Glamorous thoughts will make you tingle and fizz. You may even want to experiment with a more dangerous edge—think Kim Novac in *Vertigo*.

Set the scene

Set the scene at home—even if you're going out. A seductive sensual boudoir chez toi will make you tingle even when you're doing those last bits of washing up. Choose your music. I will leave this up to you, but go for anything that makes you feel irresistible. Leave your home in a gorgeous, welcoming state. Even if you do come home alone, it's far more glam to be greeted by order rather than piles of discarded shoes, scarves, lipsticks without lids.

Alluring eyes

Think about smoky eyes—you might want to experiment with different eye shadow—although Marlene Dietrich used carbon from a match mixed with baby oil. Wear fabrics that make your skin feel gloriously at one with its sensuality.

night out with the girls

Admit it. Getting ready with your friends for a night out is heaven sent. I have spent many an evening getting glammed up to go out with my girlfriends and when we look back on the evening, we often say that the preparation part was just as much fun as the time we spent out. I'm not saying that every time you meet up with friends you have to do the pre-evening session, but for big nights out, it's to be recommended.

Getting ready

Here are some ideas for gleeful glamour preparation:

* Invite everyone over hours before you need to get started.
* Offer plates of tropical fruit or smoothies. No alcohol yet—you'll get tired and over-emotional and your make-up will look tawdry.
* Try on a friend's clothes and feel different.
* Set up an ironing board with linen water spray for pressing, plus shoe cleaning kit and clothes brush.
* Do spa treatments on each other: manicures, head massages, etc.
* Provide a selection of face masks. Get everyone to put on a face mask then try to relax. You won't. You'll get overexcited.
* Play soothing yet upbeat music: Café del Mar and any chillout compilations are perfect.
* Pool make-up and create a zone which looks and feels professional.
* Make sure you've got limitless hot water for baths and showers.

* Light your bathroom with candles and provide bathrobes. Make sure you've got more than one hairdryer and access to more than one mirror.
* Book taxis if you need to—don't leave this until the last minute, as it'll end in tears.
* Start getting ready—dressed and made up two hours before the taxi is due to arrive—and help each other with hair and make up.
* Make Flirtinis with champagne, vodka, and raspberries. Serve them in beautiful glasses and take a group photo.

Once the preparation's complete, here are my top tips for a truly glamorous night out with the girls:

Dancing
Glamour on the dance floor doesn't come naturally to everyone. Ideally, you will go to classes in salsa, jitterbug, lindyhop, or Ceroc. Practice at home in front of the mirror by all means and ask friends for advice before you go public.

Alcohol
Cocktails, champagne, Chablis. Whatever your tipple, go easy. Glamorous girls don't trip up when they're out on the town. They don't spew up in taxis and they certainly don't end up falling in the gutter.

Drink and be merry but remember this: Did you ever see Lauren Bacall looking queasy because she'd had one too many martinis?

Flirting

Always essential but there are ways and ways. Be classy, be enigmatic, but most of all, be yourself. And for God's sake have fun. From where I'm sitting, there is far too little flirting going on these days and it's so good for the soul. So flirt and enjoy flirting.

Sleep

Get lots. There's nothing like planning a night out so that you can enjoy a real humdinger of a sleep, safe in the knowledge that you don't have to do much the next day. Unplug the home phone, turn off your cell phone, and don't set your alarm clock. Snuggle down in crisp white linen and sleep like a baby.

The morning after

Telephone debriefing is *de rigeur*. Wear your glam loafing gear, eat croissants, make smoothies, scrambled eggs, and lox, and drink herbal teas (oh, and really strong coffee if you must) as you while away the morning catching up. If you have overnight guests, make sure you feed them well and provide them with delicious products for detoxing and reviving.

formal *glamour*

For us girls, formal dressing can pose
problems. Unless you're loaded or a celeb,
that is. The formal events you get invited
to may not have the red-carpet razzmatazz
of the Oscars, but you'll still want to feel
super-confident when you walk along the
church's parking lot or the swirly carpet
in someone's house.

weddings

Don't you just love them? Personally, I love the way absolutely every guest ups the sartorial ante and looks way, way better than their best. Weddings are great for flirting—whether you go with your paramour or long-term other half—everyone is just so UP for it.

I almost feel that I don't need to advise on glamour for weddings—weddings are so glamorous and guests rarely disappoint. The same goes for christenings, it has to be said. Christenings have a real "let's put on our best threads to welcome this child into the world" spirit about them. It's as if the guests and godparents are hoping that some of their style will rub off on the baby.

One of the most marvelous things about weddings is that they are colourful occasions. Yes indeed. Have you ever been to an event with such a total absence of black? I know many evening weddings are black tie and that's a different color game altogether, but your average summer wedding is a riot of colors—largely pastel, admittedly. What a refreshing change of palette.

Given that weddings bring out the confidence and glamour expertise in all of us, need I say more? Not really. Nevertheless, here are some pointers:

Sunglasses
The bigger the better. Huge, in fact.

Shoes
Sexy. Strappy.

Gloves
Oh go on. Why not?

Hats
The bigger the better. You do need a plan for very hot days when you take off your hat to reveal a slimy egg head. Think about this carefully. If you don't want to shell out for a hat, you can always go down the fascinator route and flounce around in a light and airy, feathery way.

Coordinated
Easy does it. Too much matching says "Mother of the Bride."

Evenings
Funny how those sugared almond suits suddenly look very odd on the dance floor. I have been to weddings where the guests do three changes of clothes. It's your call—but I think you should wear whatever makes you feel fit to flirt.

premieres and awards

"I'd like to thank the Academy, I'd like to thank Miramax, I'd like to thank my mother for having me..."

I can't be sure, but I would guess that we won't be called upon to make this kind of speech more than once—if that—in our lifetime. Nevertheless, you have to be prepared. Who hasn't had to go to an industry awards dinner or even had to step in for their boss or someone higher up to attend a sparkling star-studded event? You need to feel quietly confident and not get into a sartorial spin. Popular classics for glittering prize ceremonies include:

Little black dress
Oh, all right. This is what most people wear. If you wear a little black dress (LBD), make sure you see it as a blank canvas, and be sure to glam it up. Don't be staid, cos there's nothing worse. Be noticed, don't be another bland raven in a big reception room with a disco ball.

Sequinned corset
Worn with jeans and really cool shoes this can be such a good look. And a breath of fresh air if you manage to move away from the LBD.

Tuxedo
Very Armani. Very Jodie Foster.

acknowledgments

I'd like to thank my mum for telling me tales of a more glamorous era and for sharing stories about wearing smart suits and gloves to drive down to Cornwall, England. Thank you Natasha for always being there to advise on sartorial dilemmas, and for being a constant source of inspiration! Mary, thank you for bringing sequins and overall sparkle to my life. Thank you Lawrence for sharing glamorous musings on the essence of va -va-voom. Paul, thank you for doing extremely bad Cary Grant impersonations and also for our general glamour discussions. Ruth, you continue to prove that Top Shop and other high street retail outlets can really be the home of unexpectedly glamorous purchases. Lucy, may you be gorgeous and glamorous forever. Di, you never fall short of true glamour and Laura and I will always be inspired by you. Rachel, I love your appreciation of glamour, fun, and fizz. And Sarah, thank you for being the most wonderful life coach ever!